ROYAL ACADEMY OF ARTS EXHIBITION RECORD BOOK

EBURY PRESS STATIONERY

FIRST PUBLISHED IN 1992 BY
EBURY PRESS STATIONERY
AN IMPRINT OF THE RANDOM CENTURY GROUP
RANDOM CENTURY HOUSE,
20 VAUXHALL BRIDGE ROAD,
LONDON SW1V 2SA
COPYRIGHT DESIGN © RANDOM CENTURY GROUP 1992
ILLUSTRATIONS © PROFESSOR NORMAN ADAMS RA,
WILLIAM BOWYER RA, FREDERICK GORE CBE RA,
ROGER DE GREY KCVO PRA, PAUL HOGARTH OBE RA,
MICHAEL ROTHENSTEIN RA, PHILIP SUTTON RA 1992

ALL RIGHTS RESERVED. NO PART OF THIS BOOK MAY
BE REPRODUCED IN ANY FORM OR BY ANY MEANS
WITHOUT PERMISSION IN WRITING FROM THE
PUBLISHER.

SET IN ERHARDT
BY TEK ART LTD, CROYDON, SURREY

PRINTED IN ITALY

DESIGNED BY PETER BENNETT

ISBN 0 09 175 288 4

COVER AND TITLE PAGE ILLUSTRATION:
Landscape by Frederick Gore CBE RA

Philip Sutton RA
Orange Lilies, Flowers from Morfa Terrace
(Detail)

RECORD BOOK

| EXHIBITION |

| WHERE |

| WHEN |

RECORD BOOK

EXHIBITION

EXHIBITION

William Bowyer RA
Isabella Placetation
(*Detail*)

RECORD BOOK

EXHIBITION

WHERE

WHEN

RECORD BOOK

EXHIBITION

RECORD BOOK

EXHIBITION

Roger De Grey KCVO PRA
La Tremblade
(*Detail*)

RECORD BOOK

EXHIBITION

WHERE

WHEN

RECORD BOOK

EXHIBITION

EXHIBITION

Michael Rothenstein RA
Night Butterfly
(*Detail*)

RECORD BOOK

EXHIBITION

WHERE

WHEN

RECORD BOOK

EXHIBITION

EXHIBITION

Professor Norman Adams RA
A Soul's Journey
(*Detail*)

RECORD BOOK

EXHIBITION

WHERE

WHEN

EXHIBITION

EXHIBITION

Frederick Gore CBE RA
Poppyfield Below
Lacoste 1988
(*Detail*)

RECORD BOOK

EXHIBITION

WHERE

WHEN

RECORD BOOK

EXHIBITION

EXHIBITION

Roger De Grey KCVO PRA
Marennes Canal,
Evening II
(*Detail*)

RECORD BOOK

EXHIBITION

WHERE

WHEN

RECORD BOOK

EXHIBITION

EXHIBITION

William Bowyer RA
Studio Still Life
(*Detail*)

RECORD BOOK

EXHIBITION

WHERE

WHEN

EXHIBITION

RECORD BOOK

EXHIBITION

Michael Rothenstein RA
Untitled 1990
(*Detail*)

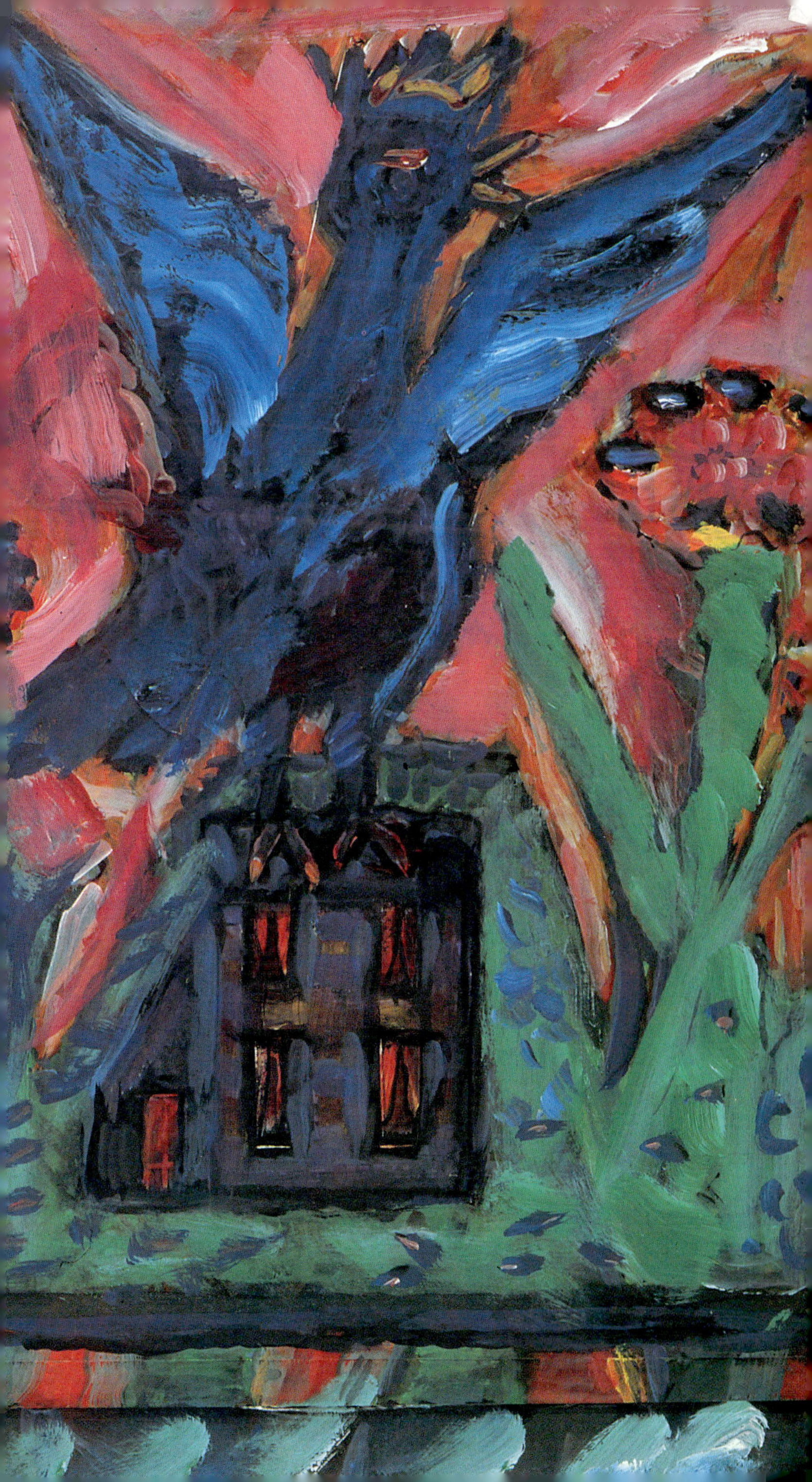

EXHIBITION

WHERE

WHEN

EXHIBITION

RECORD BOOK

EXHIBITION

Roger De Grey KCVO PRA
Ile d'Oléron
(*Detail*)

RECORD BOOK

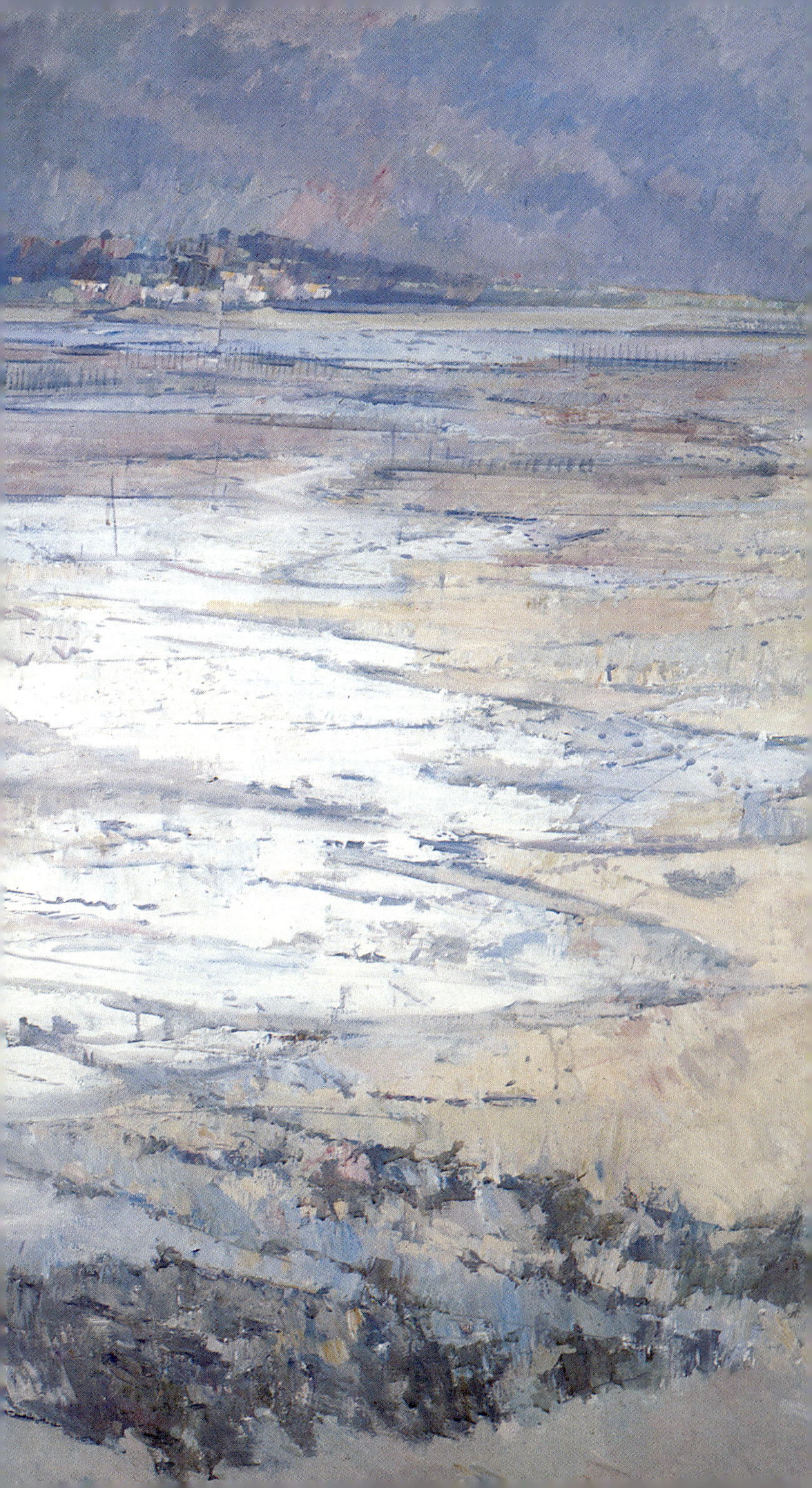

EXHIBITION

WHERE

WHEN

EXHIBITION

EXHIBITION

William Bowyer RA
Winter Reflections
(*Detail*)

RECORD BOOK

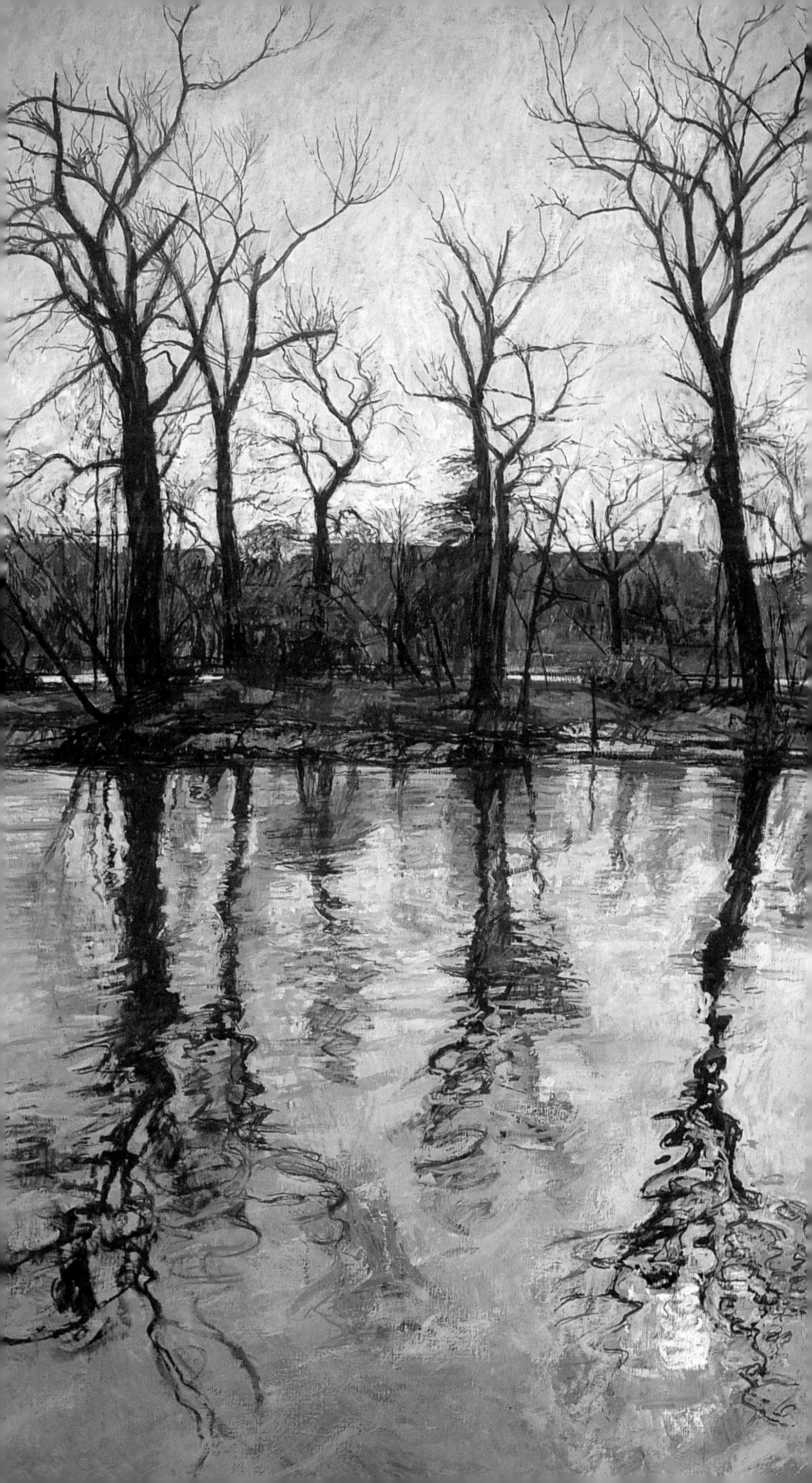

EXHIBITION

WHERE

WHEN

RECORD BOOK

EXHIBITION

RECORD BOOK

EXHIBITION

Paul Hogarth OBE RA
Georgetown,
Washington D.C.

RA
RECORD BOOK

Paul HOGARTH
The Bodisco House, O Street, Georgetown
Washington DC

EXHIBITION

WHERE

WHEN

EXHIBITION

EXHIBITION

Frederick Gore CBE RA
Geraniums on a Window Sill
(*Detail*)

RA
RECORD BOOK

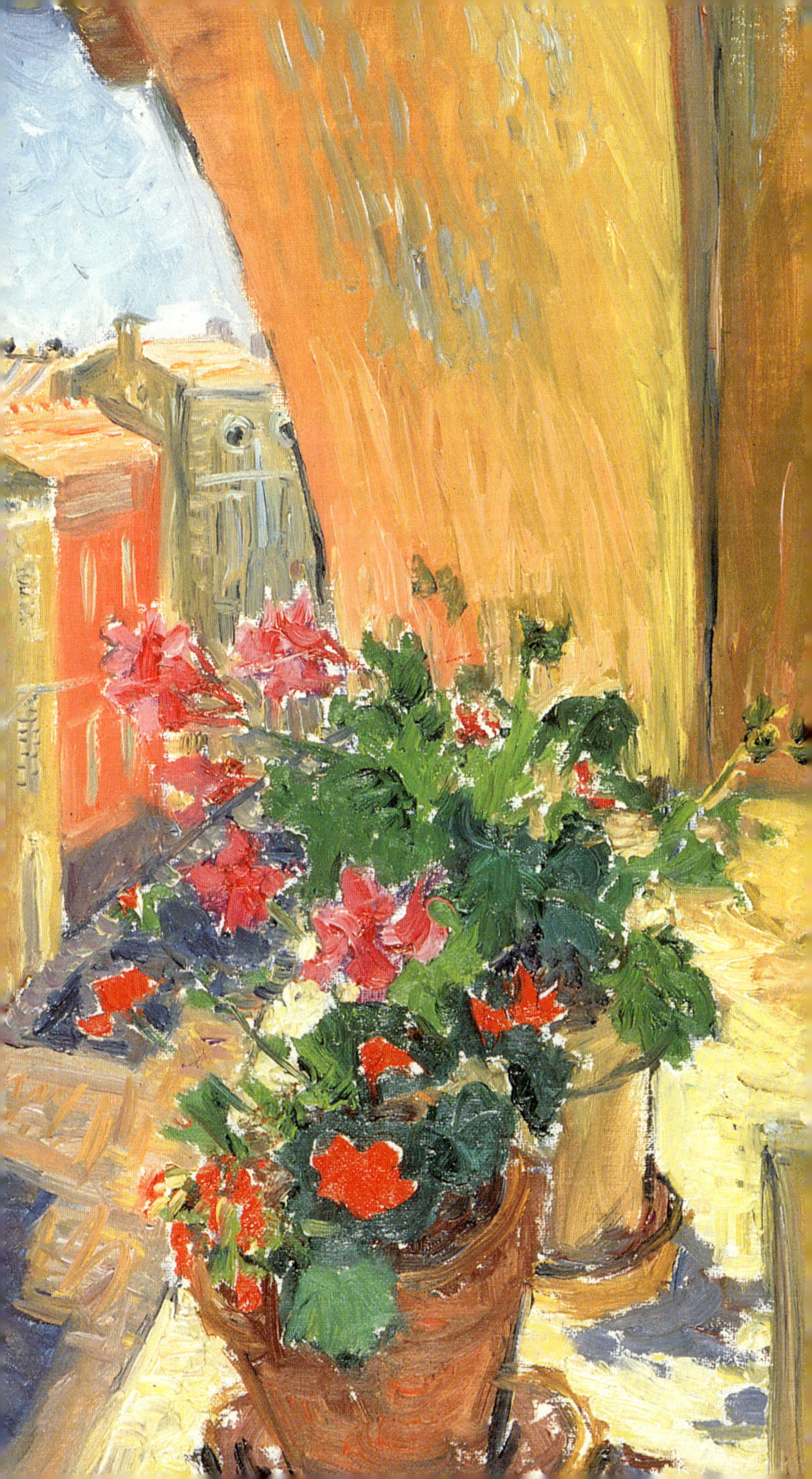

FORTHCOMING EXHIBITIONS

TITLE/ARTIST

WHERE

WHEN

TITLE/ARTIST

WHERE

WHEN

TITLE/ARTIST

WHERE

WHEN

RECORD BOOK

FORTHCOMING EXHIBITIONS

TITLE/ARTIST

WHERE

WHEN

TITLE/ARTIST

WHERE

WHEN

TITLE/ARTIST

WHERE

WHEN

FORTHCOMING EXHIBITIONS

TITLE/ARTIST

WHERE

WHEN

TITLE/ARTIST

WHERE

WHEN

TITLE/ARTIST

WHERE

WHEN

RECORD BOOK

FORTHCOMING EXHIBITIONS

TITLE/ARTIST

WHERE

WHEN

TITLE/ARTIST

WHERE

WHEN

TITLE/ARTIST

WHERE

WHEN

RECORD BOOK

FORTHCOMING EXHIBITIONS

TITLE/ARTIST

WHERE

WHEN

TITLE/ARTIST

WHERE

WHEN

TITLE/ARTIST

WHERE

WHEN

FORTHCOMING EXHIBITIONS

TITLE/ARTIST

WHERE

WHEN

TITLE/ARTIST

WHERE

WHEN

TITLE/ARTIST

WHERE

WHEN

FORTHCOMING EXHIBITIONS

TITLE/ARTIST

WHERE

WHEN

TITLE/ARTIST

WHERE

WHEN

TITLE/ARTIST

WHERE

WHEN

Roger De Grey KCVO PRA
Marennes Canal,
Evening I
(*Detail*)

RECORD BOOK

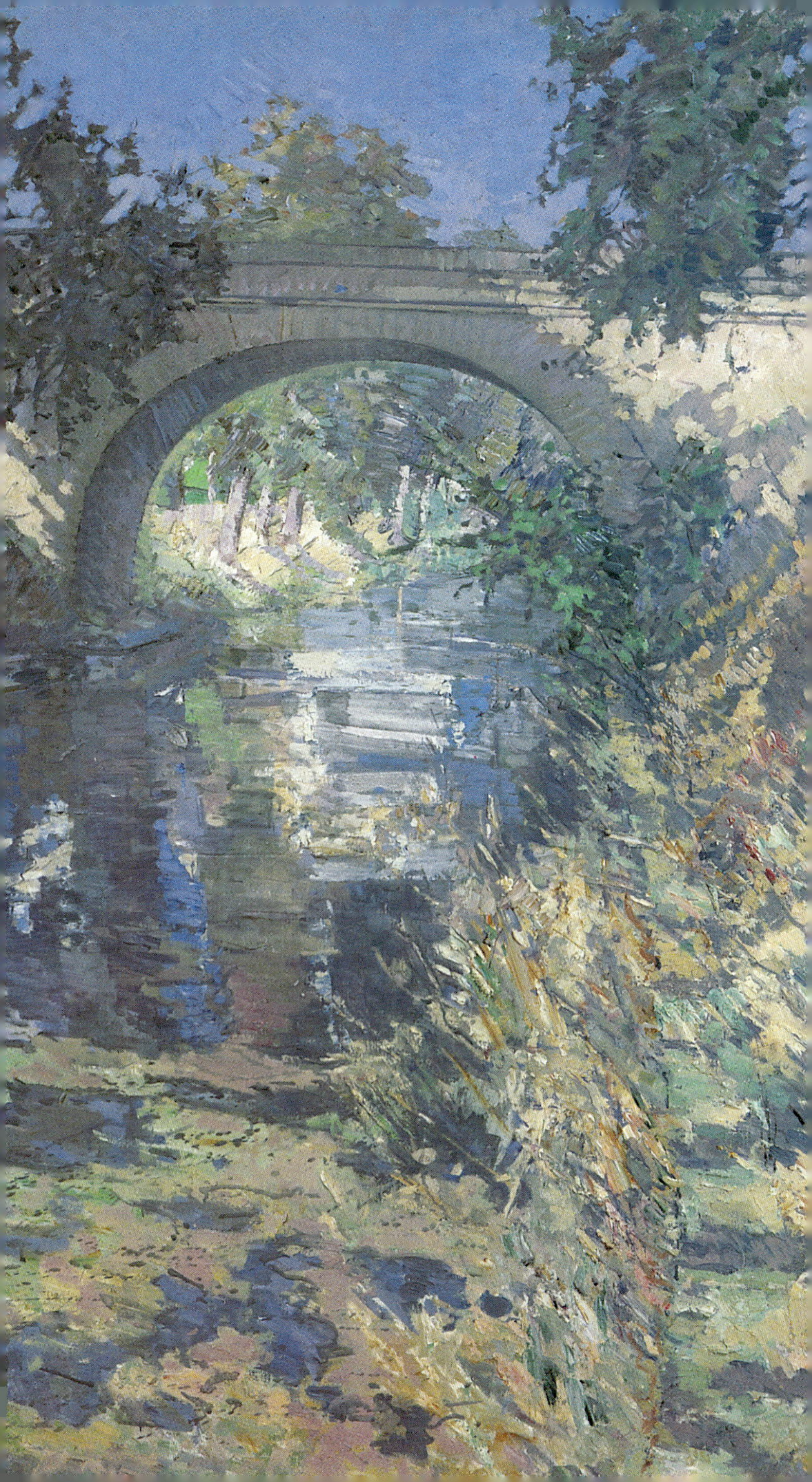

GALLERY ADDRESSES

GALLERY *Royal Academy of Arts*
Burlington House, Piccadilly, London W1V 0DS
TELEPHONE *071-439 7438*

GALLERY

TELEPHONE

GALLERY

TELEPHONE

GALLERY

TELEPHONE

GALLERY

TELEPHONE

GALLERY

TELEPHONE

GALLERY

TELEPHONE

GALLERY

TELEPHONE

GALLERY

TELEPHONE

RECORD BOOK

GALLERY ADDRESSES

GALLERY

TELEPHONE

GALLERY

TELEPHONE

GALLERY

TELEPHONE

GALLERY

TELEPHONE

GALLERY

TELEPHONE

GALLERY

TELEPHONE

GALLERY

TELEPHONE

GALLERY

TELEPHONE

GALLERY ADDRESSES

GALLERY

TELEPHONE

GALLERY

TELEPHONE

GALLERY

TELEPHONE

GALLERY

TELEPHONE

GALLERY

TELEPHONE

GALLERY

TELEPHONE

GALLERY

TELEPHONE

GALLERY

TELEPHONE

GALLERY

TELEPHONE

RECORD BOOK

GALLERY ADDRESSES

GALLERY

TELEPHONE

GALLERY

TELEPHONE

GALLERY

TELEPHONE

GALLERY

TELEPHONE

GALLERY

TELEPHONE

GALLERY

TELEPHONE

GALLERY

TELEPHONE

GALLERY

TELEPHONE

GALLERY

TELEPHONE

GALLERY ADDRESSES

GALLERY

TELEPHONE

GALLERY

TELEPHONE

GALLERY

TELEPHONE

GALLERY

TELEPHONE

GALLERY

TELEPHONE

GALLERY

TELEPHONE

GALLERY

TELEPHONE

GALLERY

TELEPHONE

GALLERY

TELEPHONE

RECORD BOOK